# The Wonderful Thursday Club

## Animal Poems

Gordon Snell is the author of The Thursday Club and more than twenty other books for children, many of them in verse. He has also written plays, song lyrics and opera librettos performed on stage, radio and television. He is married to the writer Maeve Binchy and lives near Dublin.

# The Wonderful Thursday Club

## Animal Poems

### Gordon Snell

Illustrated by Anthony Flintoft

Dolphin

First published in Great Britain in 2001
as a Dolphin Paperback
by Orion Children's Books
a division of the Orion Publishing Group Ltd
Orion House
5 Upper St Martin's Lane
London WC2H 9EA

A catalogue record for this book is available from the British Library.

Printed in Great Britain by The Guernsey Press Co. Ltd, Guernsey, C.I.

ISBN 1 84255 030 6

These tales of creatures small and great
On earth and in the skies above,
I very proudly dedicate
With all my love, to dearest Maeve.

# Contents

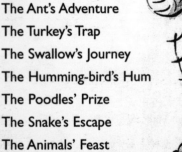

Look at the end of the section to find
the answers to the quiz poems!

# More Stories in the Forest

On a Thursday in the forest
It is storytelling time
Creatures gather in a circle
Telling stories all in rhyme.
Always on a Thursday morning
Long before the sun is high
There's an air of big excitement
And you'll hear the creatures cry:

The Thursday Club's meeting
We all want to go
What's the best way to get there?
Does anyone know?

The crab says: "Slide along sideways
Claw by claw, like me."
"Hop-hop-hop!" says the kangaroo
"Just keep buzzing around," says the bee.
"Flip your flippers," the dolphin says,
"Jump up and down," says the flea.
"Run round in circles," the greyhound barks,
"Flap your wings," squawks the bird in the tree.

"Dive from the sky," cries the eagle,
"Swim," says the salmon in the sea.

The Thursday Club's meeting
The only way to get there
Is the way you know.

If you slide or hop or run there
Or swim or jump or dive
It doesn't really matter
As long as you arrive!

Always there to choose the stories
Is Big Bill, the woolly dog.
Each storyteller he has chosen
Comes and stands upon a log.

# The First Thursday

Big Bill now will make the choice
In his deep, melodious voice...

A greedy panda starts us off
And then a goat who loves to scoff;
An elephant comes out to play
Then there's a tongue-twister to say.
A hedgehog and a fox play tricks
And then a bug is in a fix.
A puzzle and a parrot's plot,
Ants and starry skies we've got.
Tell your story, tell your rhyme,
Come and tell it, now's the time.

# The Panda's Feast

Now who could believe that a panda
Could eat quite as much as Miranda?
  She managed to chew
  Seven tons of bamboo
And then she ate up the verandah!

# The Goat's Vote

The animals were asked to vote
To say whose greed was worst.
They all declared: "We know the goat
Just has to be the first.

"Show him a cupboard, and he'll nab
Whatever's on the shelf;
The rubbish in the bin he'll grab –
Then eat the bin itself.

"He'll eat the pillows from the bed,
The mat saying *Home Sweet Home*,
The roof from off the garden shed
And every garden gnome.

"He'll chew the legs from grandma's chair,
He'll eat the baby's cot –
And to be frank, he doesn't care
If Baby's there or not.

"He'll come and munch the mobile phones
While everyone is sleeping –
Until they hear the ringing tones
Inside his stomach bleeping.

"He'll eat the seaweed on the beach,
The engines out of cars –
And if his neck could only reach,
He'd try to eat the stars.

"That goat is always guzzling –
His appetite is great.
But one thing's really puzzling:
He never puts on weight!"

# The Elephant's Game

The elephant said, feeling cocky:
"With my trunk I can learn to play hockey.
  Now it's curved like a stick
  I shall run just as quick
As a race-horse without any jockey!"

When his trunk missed the ball, he'd no fears –
He just flipped it on with his ears;
  Opponents all reeled
  As he stomped down the field
To the spectators' deafening cheers.

The elephant told them: "I bet
In goal I can do better yet."
   He did, and what's more
   No opponent could score
For his body blocked up the whole net!

The net tangled up round his head
And his tusks cut it all to a shred.
   He said: "*I've* won the Cup,
   So I'll give this game up
And I'll start to play cricket instead!"

# The Sheep's Tongue-Twister

On a slope so steep, a sheep's asleep –
See the shape of the sheep on the slope so steep.
A sparrow swoops with a shrill *cheep-cheep*
So the sheep can't sleep on the slope so steep.

# The Hedgehog's Revenge

Higgledy Piggledy Hedgehog
Was very sad and sorry
To see the friends who met their ends
All flattened by a lorry.
Higgledy Piggledy Hedgehog
Said a magic spell:
"FEE-FI-FO! I'll grow and grow!"
Then he began to swell.

Higgledy Piggledy Hedgehog –
Oh what a big surprise –
Swelled up soon like some balloon
To fifty times his size.
Higgledy Piggledy Hedgehog
Stuck out each pointed spike
And cried: "Look here, and see me spear
Just anything I like!"

Higgledy Piggledy rolled around
On the ground, round and round

Spiked a truck with a load of muck
Spiked a train and an aeroplane
Spiked a ship and a rubbish tip
Rolling round and round.

Higgledy Piggledy rolled around
On the ground, round and round

Spiked some trees and a hive of bees
Spiked a yacht and a parking lot
Spiked a ditch and a football pitch
Rolling round and round.

Higgledy Piggledy rolled around
On the ground, round and round

Spiked a tank and a high street bank
Spiked a boat and a castle moat
Spiked a tower and a rosy bower
Rolling round and round.

Higgledy Piggledy Hedgehog
Said: "Now before I stop
I shall begin to spin and spin
Just like a high-speed top."

Higgledy Piggledy Hedgehog
Went on spinning there
And all the things as if they'd wings
Flew off into the air.

Higgledy Piggledy Hedgehog
Spun round and round and round
He spun so fast until at last
He flew right off the ground.

Higgledy Piggledy Hedgehog
Went into orbit soon
And those who know can see him glow
A bit below the moon.

Higgledy Piggledy Hedgehog
Has passed the Zodiac test:
In a starry sky he's easy to spy –
He's spikier than the rest!

# The Bug's Jug

Bug in a jug
Bug in a jug
Swimming around in the drink.
He thinks he is lucky
But others say: "YUCKY!"
And pour him away down the sink.

# The Fox's Jokes

The fox just loved to play practical jokes –
There was no mad scheme that he wouldn't tackle;
And at every trick and prank and hoax
He'd roll on the ground and hoot and cackle.

He invited the stork to eat his fill
From some soup he put on a shallow plate.
The stork couldn't sip with her long thin bill
While the wily fox just ate and ate.

"Aren't you hungry, my friend? Well, that's too bad!"
The fox said slyly, and smiled with glee.
"Never mind," said the stork, "but you'll make me glad
If tomorrow you'll come and eat with *me*."

Next day the greedy fox came round
But his joky ways the stork would check
For the soup he was offered was placed, he found,
In a jar that was tall, with a narrow neck.

The stork with his bill so long and thin
Supped up the soup with slurpy sips,
But the fox's snout just wouldn't go in
And he sat there hungrily, licking his lips.

The stork said, smiling: "Not hungry, my friend?"
As the fox slunk off with an angry croak.
"Well, well!" called the stork, "it seems in the end
That our friend Mister Fox can't take a joke!"

# Scrambled Animals

The Secret Games are being held today
And the creatures' names are a big surprise;
The letters are mixed in a scrambled way
So each of them has their own disguise.

The DURIBBLE flutters its feathered wings,
The PHINDOL leaps in the rippling bay.
The SEPRID weaves, the RACANY sings,
And the STOORER crows at the dawn of day.
The SWAP stings and the GODBULL barks *bow-wow*,
The TINKET mews at the LOPAR bear.

Can you unscramble the letters now
And try to discover just who is there?

# The Parrot's Plot

Pete the parrot used to boast:
"I'm the Most, from coast to coast!
There's no creature in the nation
Who has my skill at imitation.

"I can make a noise like rain
I can imitate a train
A bull, a bear, a rattlesnake –
There is no sound I cannot make."

So Pete decided he'd have fun
By playing tricks on everyone.
First he gave out, loud and true,
A rooster's *cock-a-doodle-doo*.

But the time was far from right:
It was the middle of the night!
The other creatures with a yawn
All woke up, thinking it was dawn.

When they found that it was dark
They heard Pete chuckle: "What a lark!"
He watched them grumbling and scowling,
And then gave out a wolf-like howling.

The wolves all gathered in a pack –
They thought there must be prey to track.
They asked their leader: "Where's the hunt?
Why aren't you rushing out in front?"

He told them: "That howl woke me too –
I thought it must be one of *you*!
Being woken makes me wild."
But Pete the parrot simply smiled.

Then he gave out a gentle cooing;
A dove said: "Ah! It's time for wooing!
I'll go and find that lovelorn dove
And with a kiss I'll swear my love."

And so, with darkness all around,
He fluttered off towards the sound,
Then cried: "That's not the kiss I seek
But some sharp old ugly parrot's beak!"

Pete flew off laughing, then let loose
A sound just like a honking goose.
The geese, fooled by his imitation,
Asked: "Is it time for our migration?"

Their flight south they began to make
But soon they realised their mistake.
Just as they turned, one said: "I see
A parrot, honking in a tree!"

The angry geese all flocked around
And knocked the parrot to the ground.
Then wolves and doves and all the rest
Took their revenge with furious zest.

Afraid they'd tear him quite asunder,
Pete made a sound like roaring thunder.
The creatures stared into the sky
And Pete said quickly: "I must fly!"

He flew away, for Pete was keen
To find himself a change of scene –
Somewhere he'd try to have the patience
To cease his joky imitations.

# The Anteater's Nose

Anteater, anteater,
With your pointed bill
You poke your nose in
To our anthill.

Anteater, anteater,
With your snuffling snout
You poke your nose in
And winkle us out.

Anteater, anteater,
We think you're rude
Why don't you poke your nose in
To find some other food?

Anteater, anteater,
Let us please suggest
You go and poke your nose in
This lovely wasps' nest!

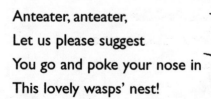

# The Stargazers

From the deep dark sky the stars shine down
On forest and sea and field and town:
Mystery lights that gleam and glow
What are the stars? Will we ever know?
Mystery lights that glow and gleam
What are the stars? We can only dream.

The starfish stated: "You must agree
That those pointed stars are a lot like *me*.
They are starfish spirits awaiting birth
And when it's time, they will come to Earth."

The firefly told them: "Those points of light
Are fireflies twinkling in the night.
There were just too many in this one place
So the fireflies conquered Outer Space!"

The glow-worm said: "Now don't you see
That the universe is a giant tree?
It arches over us, always growing
And on every branch there's a glow-worm glowing."

The panther said: "That sky so black
Is a crowd of panthers in a huddled pack.
Those stars you see are their yellow eyes
Staring down from the distant skies."

They all looked up, calling: "Tell us true –
Stars above us, just what are *you*
You mystery lights we gaze upon?"
But the stars were silent, and twinkled on.

Let's all clap our fins and claws,
Our wings, our hooves, our furry paws!
Here next week in sun or rain
The Thursday Club will meet again.

Page 26 : Scrambled Animals
BLUEBIRD, DOLPHIN, SPIDER, CANARY, ROOSTER,
WASP, BULLDOG, KITTEN, POLAR BEAR

# The Second Thursday

You've travelled over hills and dales
To tell us all your Thursday tales.

First, porpoise is a playful mammal,
And there's a rescue by a camel.
A cricket bats, and ants come out;
  A cackling turkey struts about.
A bird hums and a poodle splashes
  A big snake into hiding dashes.
There is a journey for the swallow
And then a great big feast to follow.

Tell your story, tell your rhyme,
Come and tell it, now's the time.

# The Porpoise's Purpose

The porpoise's purpose was pelting the parrot
With pancakes and pastries and pieces of paper.
When the parrot protested it just wasn't proper
The porpoise went purple and splashed him with porridge.

The parrot replied with a pan full of prune-juice
Which he poured on the porpoise with loud peals of laughter.
They splashed and they sploshed in the prune-juice and porridge
And the porpoise and parrot were friends ever after!

37

# The Camel's Rescue

The sultan's horse was a glorious creature
Fair and fine in every feature
With a jewelled saddle and a golden rein
And silken tassels on its glossy mane.

The sultan's camel was a scruffy hack
With a mangy hump upon its back.
Its legs were gangly and its teeth were yellow
And it deafened the desert with its screeching bellow.

A falcon chick was the sultan's pet
It had flown away and was not back yet.
The sultan said: "A reward there'll be
For whoever brings him back to me."

"Watch *me*!" cried the horse with a boastful neigh
And into the desert he galloped away.
The camel drank water from a giant bath
And set off plodding on the desert path.

He plodded over dune after sandy dune
By the light of the sun and the light of the moon.
He passed the horse looking far from its best
And gasping: "I'm thirsty and I'm taking a rest."

The camel heard a *cheep* in the desert air –
The chick was caught in a thorn bush there.
He set it free and said: "Perch on my hump
And we'll set off home with a bump-bump-bump."

They met the horse still flopped on the ground
Puffing and panting with a breathless sound.
The camel said as he heard him wail:
"Just tie your reins to the end of my tail."

The camel set off with the chick on his hump
Dragging the horse like a great big lump.
He plodded over dune after sandy dune
By the light of the sun and the light of the moon.

When they got back home, the horse cried: "See!
The chick's been found, all thanks to *me*!"
The camel frowned at the horse's trick;
"He's telling lies!" squeaked the falcon chick.

The chick told them all the real true story
And said the camel deserved the glory.
So the horse was banished to a tumbledown shed
And the camel had the royal stable instead.

Now the camel has robes of silver and gold
And the tale of his rescue is often told,
And now and then, with a bump-bump-bump,
The falcon goes riding on the camel's hump.

# The Cricket's Game

The cricket declared: "It's a shame
That I've got this peculiar name.
   People think all us crickets
   Must bat, and take wickets –
But football is really my game!"

# The Ant's Adventure

The busy busy ants in a line they go
To and fro, to and fro,
What are they doing? The ants must know
As they go, to and fro.

One day when the sun shone bright and fine
An ant called Annie stepped out of the line.
She said: "I'm tired of these trips we make
And I think it's time to take a break!"

She sat in the sun with her head held high
And watched the busy busy line go by.
The rest of the ants said: "It's just not done
To step out of the line and enjoy the sun.

"For busy busy ants in a line must go
To and fro, to and fro."
"Why?" asked Annie. "Does anyone know
Why we go to and fro?"

When they heard her question, the ants stopped dead
And each bumped into the one ahead.
In a great big heap they all fell flat
Saying: "Nobody's ever dared ask us that!"

Since then those ants each do their own thing,
Some knit sweaters, some dance, some sing,
Some skate, some ski, some make ice-cream,
And some like Annie just sit and dream.

Those busy busy ants no longer go
To and fro, to and fro,
And why they ever did it, they just don't know
Now there's no to and fro.

# The Turkey's Trap

Turkey staggers, turkey struts,
Turkey drives the farmyard nuts!

*"Hear me gurgle, hear me gobble,
See my neck go wobble wobble!"*

Turkey cackles, turkey clucks,
Turkey pecks the hens and ducks.

*"See me caper, see me prance,
See me do a song and dance!"*

Turkey's vicious, turkey's vain,
Turkey gives us all a pain.

*"See me claw and scratch and snap –
In your face my wings I'll flap!"*

Turkey puts us in a rage –
Lock up turkey in a cage.

Leave him there to fret and fuss
Where he cannot bother *us!*

# The Swallow's Journey

Swallow follow swiftly
Swallow we must go
Swallow follow south
Where the warm winds blow.

Swallows flying southward
Seeking out the sun
Swallows sleeping soundly
When the journey's done.

# The Humming-bird's Hum

Now the humming-bird is coming –
You will find his song is fine
If you make the sound of humming
With the **m**'s that end the line.

Humming-bird, I hear you hummmmmmm...
On the air your wings you drummmmmmm...
This is how you make that hummmmmmm...
Did you learn it from your mummmmmmm...?

The humming-bird is like a rainbow,
Colours gleaming in the sky
Red as rubies, green as emeralds,
Like a jewel flying by.

Humming-bird, I hear you hummmmmmm...
On the air your wings you drummmmmmm...
This is how you make that hummmmmmm...
Did you learn it from your mummmmmmm...?

The humming-bird is like a dancer
Dazzling with each dart and dive
From the flowers it sips the nectar
Sweet as honey from the hive.

Humming-bird, I hear you hummmmmmm...
On the air your wings you drummmmmmm...
This is how you make that hummmmmmm...
Did you learn it from your mummmmmmm...?

47

# The Poodles' Prize

Peg the poodle had a pup
With curly hair and big brown eyes.
She said: "I'm going to dress her up
And then she'll win the dog-show prize."

She brushed the pup from head to paws
And tied a ribbon on her tail.
With frilly collar, polished claws
And silken coat, she couldn't fail!

But at the show the poodle pup
Looked all her rivals up and down.
She said: "I think this dressing-up
Makes each of us look like a clown."

The others said: "She's right, you know!"
And gathered in a secret huddle;
And then they dashed outside the show
And started splashing in a puddle.

Their mothers stared with saddened eyes –
They knew no prizes would be won.
Poodles in puddles get no prize
But oh, they have a lot more fun!

49

# The Snake's Escape

Saint Patrick came to Ireland
And all the snakes he banished.
  He faced them and chased them
   And dogged them and flogged them
Till into the ocean they vanished.

But one giant serpent fooled him –
Making sure it wasn't found
  It wormed and it squirmed
   And it wiggled and squiggled
And buried itself in the ground.

A hundred miles it measured
From its tail up to its mouth.
  It curved and it swerved
   Twisting round underground
As it stretched from the north to the south.

For years that snake lay hidden –
In deepest sleep it slumbered;
  And time passed till at last
  With a shake, wide awake
From its hiding place it lumbered.

It slid into the ocean
A serpent on the move
  And next day where it lay
  People found in the ground
A hundred-mile-long groove.

Water quickly filled it
With ripples all a-quiver.
  That waterway is here today –
  So long, so wide, it's Ireland's pride
And it's called the Shannon River!

# The Animals' Feast

We're all going off to the animals' feast
With a quack and a bark and a roar and a bray
And we'll have a great party with each bird and beast
And we'll gobble and guzzle and gabble all day!

The penguin will waddle, the spider will dance
With a quack and a bark and a roar and a bray
The parrot will screech and the antelope prance
And we'll gobble and guzzle and gabble all day!

The panda will paddle, the leopard will prowl
With a quack and a bark and a roar and a bray
The jackal will juggle, the dingo will howl
And we'll gobble and guzzle and gabble all day!

The chipmunk will chatter, the lyre-bird will strum
With a quack and a bark and a roar and a bray
The wombat will warble, the deer play the drum
And we'll gobble and guzzle and gabble all day!

The bear will blow bubbles, the cricket will croon
With a quack and a bark and a roar and a bray
And you can come too, if you bring a balloon –
And we'll gobble and guzzle and gabble all day!

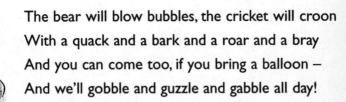

Let's all clap our fins and claws,
Our wings, our hooves, our furry paws!
Here next week in sun or rain
The Thursday Club will meet again.

# The Third Thursday

Thursday's here, so take the stage:
Storytelling's all the rage!

A shark has goldfish turning pale,
There are cuckoos, and a peacock's tale.
A stag trips, and seahorses race.
We've puzzles, and raven's chase.
A walrus stings, woodpecker knocks;
A kitten's hiding in a box.

Tell your story, tell your rhyme,
Tell your story, now's the time.

# The Shark's Ark

The Ark was standing on the harbour mud
Ready to sail on the coming Flood.
The animals went in two by two
And a pair of goldfish joined the queue.

The goldfish looked around to find
Two grinning sharks not far behind.
The goldfish shivered and stared wide-eyed
And in a shaky voice they cried:

*Let in the giraffe, he'll give us a laugh,*
*Let in the pig, he can dance a jig,*
*But don't let the shark in the Ark!*

*Let in the whale, he can tell a tale,*
*Let in the goat, though he'll chew the boat,*
*Let in the goose and the long-horned moose*
*But don't let the shark in the Ark!*

Let in the adder, he can climb the ladder,
Let in the horse, though he's rather coarse,
Let in the worm, he can only squirm,
Let in the hare and the grizzly bear
But don't let the shark in the Ark!

Let in the bat and the cat and the rat
The frog and the dog and the mouse and the louse
The mole and the vole and the owl and the fowl
And the flea and the bee and the manatee
And the shrew and the gnu and the cockatoo
But don't let the shark in the Ark!

When the sharks went in, the goldfish cried:
"If they're in there, we'll stay outside –
And we'll be safer on the whole
If we're inside a goldfish bowl!"

So when the Ark, that sturdy boat,
Upon the Flood began to float
Seeking the land it hoped to find,
It towed a goldfish bowl behind!

# The Cuckoo's Tongue-Twister

The cocky cuckoo cooked a cake
Cracked an egg to help it bake
Spilled some syrup, slipped and fell
And cracked his cuckoo head as well.

The chubby chick who took a look
Cheeped: "That cuckoo cannot cook
And this cheery chick can tell
The cuckoo's cookbook will not sell!"

COOK
CUCKOO'S
CAKES

# The Peacock's Tale

The peacock liked to strut about
And fluff his dazzling feathers out.
He fanned his tail for all to see
And shouted proudly: "Look at *me*!"

His patterned feathers, glowing bright,
Were truly an amazing sight.
The plain brown peahen was his mate;
He asked her: "Don't you think I'm great?"

"Of course you are, my dear," said she.
She found it simpler to agree,
For as the boastful peacock's wife
She liked to lead a quiet life.

The peacock said: "This tail of mine
So very colourful and fine
Ought to be seen both near and far.
I'm going to be a singing star!"

But when he opened wide his beak
A noise like some old witch's shriek
Came screeching loudly through the air
And deafened listeners everywhere.

The angry peacock flapped his tail
And went to see the nightingale.
He said: "It seems my voice won't do –
So teach me how to sing like you."

The nightingale said: "You're a bird
Whose true voice really should be heard.
I'll tell you how it can be done –
Waggle your feathers one by one.

"Whichever feather is your choice
Will send a signal to your voice.
Each makes a different note, and soon
You're singing a melodious tune."

The peacock tried it, but he found
He still gave out that screeching sound.
"I'll show you," said the nightingale.
"Lend me the feathers from your tail."

Although he had a little doubt
The peacock let her pluck them out.
She stuck them in her own tail then
And cried: "You won't see *those* again!

"My costume will be all the rage
When I go on the opera stage.
It really was a foolish thing
To think that feathers help you sing!

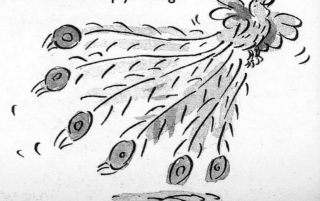

"They're beautiful – and now I've got 'em
You'll have to live with your bare bottom!"
Singing a song, away she flew.
The peacock cried: "What can I do?"

The peahen said: "Stay in the den
Until your feathers grow again.
They were your glory, truth to tell –
Why did you want to sing as well?"

"The nightingale who said she'd school you
Knew by your vanity she'd fool you.
Hide your behind, and hang your head –
*I'll* strut about the place instead!"

63

# The Stag's Antlers

A stag said, gazing into a pool:
"I rather admire that reflection of mine.
I'm not very boastful – well, not as a rule –
But I've never seen antlers that look so fine."

He strutted about like a turkey cock
Waving his antlers round and round.
With his horns in the air, he tripped on a rock
And fell in a heap on the stony ground.

He cried: "I'm hurt, and I can't stand now,"
And he pierced the air with his grunts and squeals.
Some passing sparrows said: "Stop that row!
You'll just have to lie there until it heals."

As he grumbled, the sparrows said: "Stop your fuss –
Look on the bright side, you're safe from stalking;
And think how useful you'll be to *us* –
We can use your antlers for tightrope walking!"

They tied on strings, and they pranced about –
The stag's dark eyes with rage were glowing.
"You've learned," said the sparrows, "without a doubt:
Even vain creatures should look where they're going!"

# The Seahorses' Race

When Sam the seahorse raised his head
A fine sight met his eyes –
Along the beach, racehorses sped
Competing for a prize.

So when he dived below once more
Sam had a tale to tell:
"Those horses race upon the shore –
Why can't we race as well?

"A seahorse race, that's what we need –
Our skills will be revealed
As crowds of fish cheer on each steed
Who gallops round the field.

"So here's the starting-gate," said Sam,
"Now all line up with me.
A champion, that's what I am!
Let's gallop through the sea."

Sam stumbled as he tottered off –
The others wobbled after.
The watching whales began to scoff,
The lobsters roared with laughter.

The dogfish barked: "That's surely not
The way a real horse moves.
That lot can't gallop, walk or trot –
They've got no legs or hooves!"

The ocean creatures rocked with mirth
To see Sam's mad plan fail,
For nobody on sea or earth
Can gallop, with a tail!

Sam didn't take their scorn to heart
For still he had a dream.
He said: "Instead I plan to start
A water-polo team."

And what a huge success they made
Though they were just beginners
For now, when water-polo's played
The seahorse team are winners!

# Square Animals

Now we have a Puzzle Square –
You'll find a lot of creatures there.
Look at the list that's down below;
Search up and down, and to and fro
Then look diagonally too
And you'll discover quite a few!

Look for:-

GORILLA, BEE, BAT, SWAN, TURKEY, SNAKE, LION,
TOAD, LEOPARD, CAMEL, DROMEDARY, OCTOPUS,
ASP, GERBIL, DINGO, IGUANA, OCELOT, BISON,
SHARK, ANT, GOAT, PUMA, DEER, SEAGULL, CARP,
DRAGONFLY, GRASSHOPPER, COCKROACH, YAK.

| | | | | | | | | | | | |
|---|---|---|---|---|---|---|---|---|---|---|---|
| G | O | R | I | L | L | A | X | Z | E | E | B |
| E | R | X | B | A | T | N | A | W | S | S | X |
| R | Z | A | I | X | Z | T | U | R | K | E | Y |
| B | X | X | S | N | A | K | E | Z | H | A | L |
| I | Z | Z | O | S | S | X | X | C | Z | G | F |
| L | I | O | N | X | H | G | A | Z | D | U | N |
| X | G | O | Z | D | A | O | T | X | E | L | O |
| D | U | C | X | D | R | A | P | O | E | L | G |
| I | A | E | Z | K | K | T | X | P | R | C | A |
| N | N | L | C | A | M | E | L | U | E | A | R |
| G | A | O | Y | R | A | D | E | M | O | R | D |
| O | C | T | O | P | U | S | Z | A | S | P | J |

# The Raven's Trick

In earliest times, the legends say
The world had got no light.
There was no sun, no dawn, no day
But only darkest night.

The raven hated all the dark
So thick around his perch
So he decided to embark
Upon a dangerous search.

He heard there was a secret cave
Where entry was forbidden
And there, deep down beneath the wave
A ball of light was hidden.

The raven found the secret place
But guarding it he saw
A monster with a grisly face
And sharp teeth in his jaw.

The raven boldly said to him:
"Let's go in, where it's dry.
Then you can teach me how to swim
And I'll teach *you* to fly!"

They went inside and climbed a ledge;
The raven said: "Take care –
Just raise your fins, jump off the edge
And you will fly through air!"

The monster jumped, then gave a shout
For he had got a shock:
He fell straight down and lay, knocked out,
Unconscious on a rock.

Deep in the cave the raven stole
And found the story right:
There, hidden gleaming in a hole,
He saw the ball of light.

He cradled it beneath his wing –
Into the sky he vanished.
Light to the world he meant to bring
So darkness would be banished.

An eagle saw him flying there
And swooped to grab the ball.
The raven dropped it – through the air
They watched its dazzling fall.

It split in pieces – very soon
They saw them, one by one,
Become the shining stars and moon:
The largest made the sun.

And that is how, the legends say,
The raven brought us light,
And why the sun lights up the day,
The moon and stars the night.

# The Walrus's Sting

A walrus was swimming at dusk
When a jellyfish stuck to his tusk.
   It stung and it stung
    Till it swelled up his tongue –
Now all he can eat is a rusk!

# The Woodpecker's Knock

The woodpecker said: *Knock! Knock!*
"Who's there?" said a passing flea,
"I wonder who just said *Knock! Knock!?*"
And the woodpecker said: "It's *me!*"

Said the flea: "When you say *Knock! Knock!*
'Who's there?' is the right reply.
So I say: 'Who's there?' when you knock,"
And the woodpecker said: "It's *I!*"

Said the flea: "When you say *Knock! Knock!*
'Who's there?' is your joky cue,
So I'll say 'Who's there?' when you knock,"
And the woodpecker said: "It's *you!*"

The flea said: "I fear *Knock! Knock!*
Is a joke you can never share.
From now on, when you say *Knock! Knock!*
You will find there is no one there!"

# A Kitten Called Chocs

Jenny got a chocolate box
And a kitten too.
Jenny said: "I'll call him Chocs,
And how he'll purr and mew!"

*Then she said: "I'll put my socks
In the empty chocolate box."*

One day when she called his name
And wondered to herself: "Where is he?"
Chocs the kitten never came –
Everyone was in a tizzy.

*Where was Chocs? Where was Chocs?
Sleeping in the box of socks.*

How the chickens squawked and flapped,
The geese all started hissing
And how the little puppies yapped
The day that Chocs went missing!

*Where was Chocs? Where was Chocs?*
*Sleeping in the box of socks.*

The bull did roar, the horses neighed,
The hounds they started baying.
The ducks all quacked, the donkey brayed,
The day that Chocs went straying.

*Where was Chocs? Where was Chocs?*
*Sleeping in the box of socks.*

Next morning, still no sign of Chocs;
"Where is he?" Jenny said.
Then reaching for a pair of socks
She picked out Chocs instead!

*Where was Chocs? Where was Chocs?*
*Sleeping in the box of socks.*

How everyone rejoiced and cheered,
Their happy hearts were leaping
Now Chocs the kitten had appeared –
And where had he been sleeping?

*Where was Chocs? Where was Chocs?*
*Sleeping in the box of socks!*

Let's all clap our fins and claws,
Our wings, our hooves, our furry paws
Here next week in sun or rain
The Thursday Club will meet again.

# The Fourth Thursday

Thursday's here, so gather round:
Storytellers must be found.

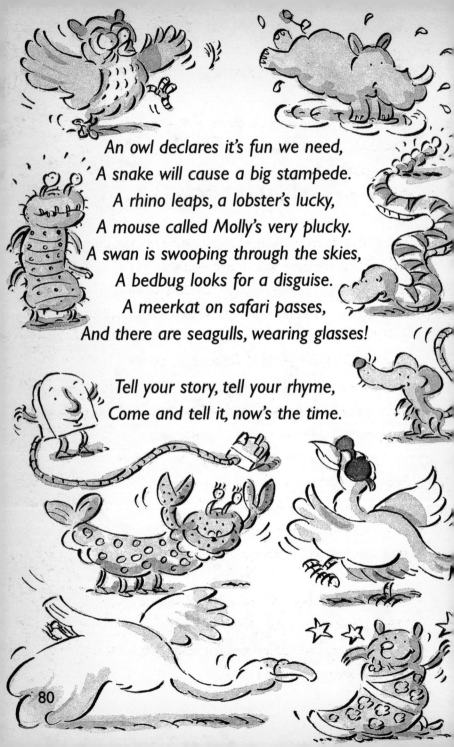

An owl declares it's fun we need,
A snake will cause a big stampede.
A rhino leaps, a lobster's lucky,
A mouse called Molly's very plucky.
A swan is swooping through the skies,
A bedbug looks for a disguise.
A meerkat on safari passes,
And there are seagulls, wearing glasses!

Tell your story, tell your rhyme,
Come and tell it, now's the time.

# The Owl's Antics

"I'm meant to be ever so clever and wise,"
The owl in the oak tree said.
"But today I shall give them all a surprise
And be ever so foolish instead."

She waggled her wings and she jumped up and down
And rolled her eyes round and round;
Then she did a big somersault just like a clown
And fell flat on her face on the ground.

She painted her face to look like a ghost
And howled like a wolf at the moon.
She juggled with jam-jars and pieces of toast
And made little mud-pies with a spoon.

She sang a loud song with ridiculous words
And she did a ridiculous dance.
Her antics astonished the rest of the birds
And shocked all her uncles and aunts.

She bowed to them all, and she said with a smile:
"The wisest bird under the sun
Must fool around sometimes, for once in a while
It really is wise to have fun!"

# The Rattlesnake's Round-up

The rattlesnake said: "It's a battle
Not to be squashed by the cattle
   So if ever I need
   To start a stampede
I just give a shake of my rattle!"

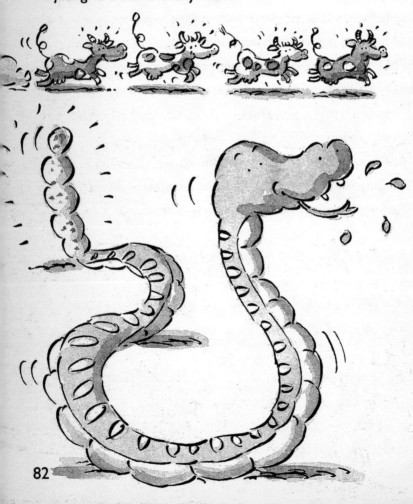

# Animal Games

And now it is time for the Animal Games –
We give you the clues and you find out the names!

My First is a snake that will squeeze, squash and squirm
My Second's a measurement, making a worm.
My Third is a creature that lays golden eggs
My Fourth has got short wings and long gangly legs.
My Fifth hoots at night in the sky as it roams
My Sixth is the place where the birds make their homes.

When you know them, take the first letter of each
And put them together, the answer to reach.

# The Rhinoceros's Leap

When Ray Rhinoceros was born
They all admired her pointy horn
    But as she grew
    She felt she knew
She should have been a unicorn.

And so one day she spent some hours
Roaming the meadows, picking flowers.
    When they were spread
    Around her head
She called upon her magic powers.

"Now like the unicorn I'll fly
With dainty hooves around the sky."
    She climbed the tree
    And said: "Watch *me*!
Among the clouds I'll soar so high."

But when she took the giant leap
She fell, and landed in a heap.
    Her heavy weight
    Was just so great
She made a crater ten feet deep.

And when the rains came, they did make
The crater into one big lake.
   The rhinos dash
   To splish and splash
And happily their thirst they slake.

They said to Ray: "Now don't be cross –
The unicorn was no great loss.
   You've made a pool
   To keep us cool –
Enjoy being a rhinoceros!"

# The Lobster's Lucky Day

Little Lily, a lonely young lobster,
Was so tearful they called her a *sobster*.
Lily soon came across
A big gangster boss –
Now she's called *Lily Lobster the Mobster!*

# The Mouse's Adventure

One night when the children had all gone home
A mouse called Molly came through the gloom
And twitching her whiskers she started to roam
Around the school's computer room.

She heard a sound like a *click-click-click*
But what it was she just couldn't tell.
Then a voice said: "Come here and I'll show you a trick;
You ought to know *I'm* a mouse as well!

"A computer mouse I am proud to be:
Look at the pictures I put on the screen,
And the words and numbers – you must agree
Such a magical mouse you've never seen."

"Well, golly!" said Molly, "what a wonderful show –
In all my life I've seen nothing cuter."
The computer mouse said: "There's a problem, though –
I'm chained by a wire to this computer.

"Would you do me a favour and set me free?
Just pull that plug out of this machine."
So Molly did, saying: "Yours has to be
The longest tail I have ever seen!"

Molly took her new-found friend with pride
On a wander round in the dead of night.
They were chased by a cat – the computer mouse cried:
"It nearly gave me a mega-bite!"

He almost drowned when he fell in a drain,
Ate a poison pellet and spat it out.
By a cheese-filled trap he was almost slain –
And he wailed: "There's danger all about."

He said: "Thank you Molly for being my tutor
But I'm safer far in my old domain.
So when we get back to my computer
Will you kindly plug me in again?"

Next day the girl who was sitting there
Clicked on the mouse with skilful ease
And was puzzled to smell, when she sniffed the air,
The faintest whiff of mousetrap cheese.

And as for Molly, she went off home
Thinking about all the things she'd seen,
And she knew very well she'd rather roam
Than be wired for ever to some machine!

# The Swan's Tongue-Twister

Silly swan, swooping slow and shyly,
Sees her swan-shaped shadow on the shore.
She is sure she's seen a second swan there —
What a strange surprise she has in store!

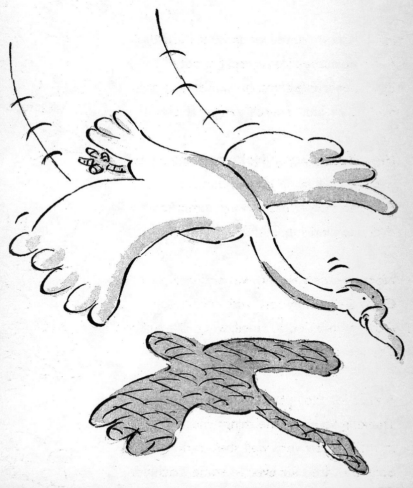

# The Bedbug's Disguise

The bedbug said: "It's my delight
To hide in someone's bed and bite!
But other insects feel they must
Regard a bedbug with disgust.

"I think the reason they're appalled
Is just the nasty name I'm called.
Even the spiders, ants and lice
Think bedbugs really are not nice.

"So now I'm using, I proclaim,
My scientific Latin name.
You insects, all with names so various,
Must call *me* CIMEX LECTULARIUS!"

Alas, the others simply laughed –
They thought his Latin name was daft.
They said: "Though you may fret and fuss
BEDBUG you'll always be, to *us*!

"Your way of life is, as we claim,
Just as disgusting as your name!
In fact, we'd find it quite hilarious
To call you CIMEX LECTULARIUS!"

The bedbug sadly shook his head
And burrowed back into the bed.

# The Meerkat's Safari

In the desert they call Kalahari
Where the African night is so starry
   A meerkat remarked:
   "It is time I embarked
On a really exciting safari."

To India that meerkat was faring;
When she came home, the others were staring;
   She returned from safari
   Dressed up in a sari –
Now it's what every meerkat is wearing!

# The Seagull's Song

An owl gazed hard at a seagull
And said with great surprise:
"It amazes me you can even see –
You've got such mean little eyes!

"They're like little black buttons
Little black specks
Little black berries
A sparrow pecks!"

"Shut your fat beak!" snapped the seagull,
"Or I'll make a meal of *you*!"
But in a mirror he took a sneaky little look
And he thought it might be true!

Eyes like little black buttons?
Little black specks?
Little black berries
A sparrow pecks?

"I know what I'll do," said the seagull,
"Dark glasses will go far
To hide my eyes in a fine disguise
And I'll look like a movie star!

   "With shiny dark glasses
   Flashy and smart
   With shiny dark glasses
   I'll look the part."

The gulls who saw that seagull
Strutting with a scornful smile
Said: "We each need a pair of those to wear
Then we'll all strut about in style.

   "With shiny dark glasses
   Flashy and smart
   With shiny dark glasses
   We'll look the part."

How they swaggered, that gang of seagulls
As they smiled and strutted by.
But their moment of glory was a different story
When they all began to fly.

  With their shiny dark glasses
  The world looked grey
  Through their shiny dark glasses
  They couldn't see the way.

They bumped into each other, those seagulls,
And into every cliff and wall
And they all grew thinner for they had no dinner
And they caught no fish at all.

  They threw away their shiny dark glasses
  And now if you walk the shore
  And you see a heap of shiny dark glasses –
  They're the ones those seagulls wore!

# Storytelling Never Ends

Let's all clap our fins and claws,
Our wings, our hooves, our furry paws!
Here next week in sun or rain
The Thursday Club will meet again.
Storytelling never ends –
So till next Thursday, farewell friends!

Page 83 : Animal Games
Python, Inch-worm, Goose, Emu, Owl, Nest
= **PIGEON**